A very special gift

Learning Unlimited's
'Literacy for Active Citizenship' series

Written by Erica Tate

A very special gift
© Learning Unlimited 2018

Published by Learning Unlimited.

Foreword

Learning Unlimited's
'Literacy for Active Citizenship' series

The graded readers in the 'Literacy for Active Citizenship' series are primarily for adults who are settling in the UK, who are speakers of other languages (ESOL) and who are still developing their skills in English and in reading.

The first 20 titles in this series were produced as part of the EU-funded Active Citizenship and English (ACE) project (July 2013 – June 2015), led by Learning Unlimited. The ACE project supported migrant women to develop their skills and confidence in English and to take an active part in everyday life in the UK. We wanted to use the real-life experiences of our learners and volunteers in a writing strand of the project to support adult migrants settling in the UK. These stories, written by learners and volunteers, include funny, personal and less typical aspects of everyday life in the UK.

Additional titles in this series have also been written by learners and volunteers from Learning Unlimited's programmes. These include stories about more serious topics such as crime and health.

We hope you enjoy the 'Literacy for Active Citizenship' series. All the stories have been edited by ESOL specialists at Learning Unlimited. There are two versions of each story – Entry 1 (A1) and Entry 2+ (A2+), each with with free downloadable supporting materials:
www.learningunlimited.co/publications/esolreaders

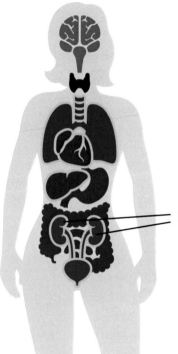

KIDNEYS

My name is Erica. I have one brother and five sisters. Four of us have polycystic kidneys. This is a kidney disease we inherited from our mother.

Doctors told me I had the same condition when I was 25 years old. They told me it was dangerous for me to have children. But I had a beautiful baby boy. He is now 28 years old.

My mother died of polycystic kidneys. My brother has had two kidney transplants.One of my sisters had a kidney transplant 10 years ago and is well.

I have a sister in the USA. She cannot
have a kidney transplant because her
health insurance cannot pay for it.
She has been sick for 20 years and
cannot get out of bed now.

When I was 54 years old, my kidneys stopped working. Doctors told me I needed a kidney transplant. This operation would give me a kidney from someone who had died.

When I was waiting for my kidney
transplant I had to spend three days
a week in hospital having dialysis.
I was very tired and did not feel well.

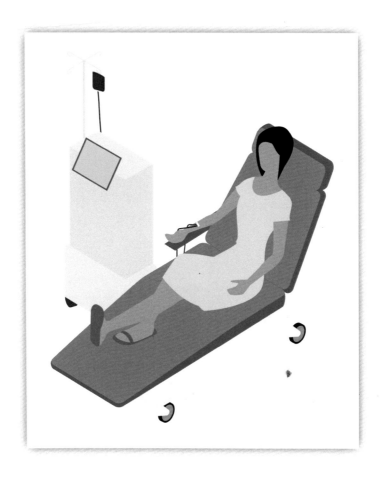

Then someone who carried a donor card died. A donor card tells doctors that they can use this person's organs to help someone who needs them.

Doctors did a kidney transplant operation. I was very lucky to get a new kidney. I feel much better now. I call my new kidney Patrick.

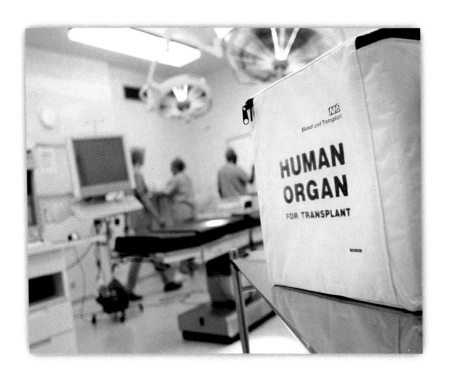

I have to take a lot of medicine and I have to see doctors at the hospital very often. I hope Patrick continues to work inside me for a long time.

I am very lucky. Someone gave me the
gift of life by giving me their kidney.
If you agree to donate an organ, you
can give someone the gift of life, too.

To find out more about organ donation, see:
www.organdonation.nhs.uk

Key words

condition	illness
dialysis	cleaning your blood with a machine
donate	to give some money or something to help other people
donor card	a card that tells doctors that when you die you want to give your organs to other people
gift	a present from someone
inherit	get something from someone in your family
kidneys	an organ that cleans the blood
organ	a part of the body which helps your body to work e.g. heart, lungs, liver
polycystic kidneys	a disease that damages the kidneys

Questions

1. What condition did Erica inherit from her mother?

2. Why did doctors tell Erica that she should not have children?

3. How old was Erica when her kidneys stopped working?

4. How did Erica feel before her kidney transplant?

5. How did Erica feel after her kidney transplant?

Talk in pairs:

6. Would you like to donate your organs when you die? Why? Why not?

7. If you needed an organ transplant, would you have one?

8. Talk about a time when someone close to you, was ill and got better.

Activity 1

Write a few sentences about a time when someone close to you was ill and got better.

How did he/she feel?

Did he/she see a doctor?

Who went to visit him/her?

Did he/she receive any gifts?

What helped him/her to get better?

How long did it take for him/her to feel better?

Activity 2

Best gifts

Work with a partner. Talk about your best gifts:

- What is the best gift you gave someone. Why was it the best?

- What is the best gift you received from someone. Why was it the best?

Report back what you have found out about best gifts.

Acknowledgements

A very special gift was written by Erica Tate. We are grateful to Erica and her family, and the NHS BT image library for being able to include some of their photographs in this book.

A very special gift was edited by Karen Dudley, Judy Kirsh, Julia McGerty and Foufou Savitzky at Learning Unlimited.

Images: iStock p.1, 6, Erica Tate, p.1, 2, 10, NHSBT image library p. 5, 7, 8
Cover images: iStock and NHSBT image library

Designed by Daisy Dudley www.daisydudley.com